A DAY in the LIFE of the DESERT

6 DESERT HABITATS, 108 SPECIES, AND HOW TO SAVE THEM

ROXIE MUNRO

holiday house • new york

To my dear editor friend, fellow Texan Rue Judd,
who cares deeply about Earth's plants and animals

A **Books for a Better Earth**™ Title

The Books for a Better Earth™ collection is designed to inspire young people to become active, knowledgeable participants in caring for the planet they live on. Focusing on solutions to climate change challenges, the collection looks at how scientists, activists, and young leaders are working to safeguard Earth's future.

Printed and bound in May 2024 at C&C Offset, Shenzhen, China.
The art was created with acrylic and India inks on archival paper.
This book was printed on FSC®-certified text paper.
www.holidayhouse.com
First hardcover edition published in 2023
First paperback edition published in 2024
3 5 7 9 10 8 6 4 2

Library of Congress Cataloging-in-Publication Data is available.

Names: Munro, Roxie, author.
Title: A day in the life of a desert : 6 desert habitats, 108 species, and how to save them / Roxie Munro.
Description: First edition. | New York : Holiday House, [2023] | Includes bibliographical references. | Audience: Ages 4–8 | Audience: Grades 2–3
Summary: "Tour 6 North American deserts in 24 hours from day break in the Mojave Desert through midnight in the Great Basin while learning about why these deserts are in danger and how to save them" – Provided by publisher.
Identifiers: LCCN 2022038639 | ISBN 9780823450923 (hardcover)
Subjects: LCSH: Desert ecology–United States–Juvenile literature. Desert animals–Habitat–United States–Juvenile literature. Deserts–United States–Juvenile literature.
Classification: LCC QH541.5.D4 M86 2023 | DDC 577.54–dc23/eng/20221202
LC record available at https://lccn.loc.gov/2022038639

ISBN: 978-0-8234-5092-3 (hardcover)
ISBN: 978-0-8234-5890-5 (paperback)

GREAT BASIN
DEATH VALLEY
MOJAVE
PAINTED DESERT
U.S.A.
SONORAN
PACIFIC OCEAN
MEXICO
CHIHUAHUAN

INTRODUCTION

We often think of a desert as a hot, arid, and uninhabitable place.

Arid? Yes. Desert precipitation is, on an average, less than ten inches a year.

Hot? Yes and no. Deserts often reach scorching temperatures of over a hundred degrees during the day, but can be quite chilly at night. And there are cold deserts—in fact, Antarctica is sometimes considered a desert!

Uninhabitable? Not at all. Though there are few large animals that can withstand the heat or make do with so little water, deserts are full of life—mostly reptiles, insects, birds, and small burrowing rodents, as well as many unique plants.

The animal residents have adapted to the desert: many live without ever drinking water, manage to avoid the sun, and have colors or patterns that help them blend in with the landscape or reflect instead of absorb heat.

At night, the desert becomes a whole different world. Many creatures are nocturnal—they come out after dark, when it cools down. Lots of animals are diurnal—busy during the day.

However, deserts are fragile ecosystems. Vegetation grows very slowly, and once disturbed can take centuries to recover. Entire animal populations that depend upon this ecosystem can be wiped out. Many of the special plants and unique animals that have adapted to live and thrive under what seem like harsh and inhospitable conditions are in trouble now. Damage from increasing

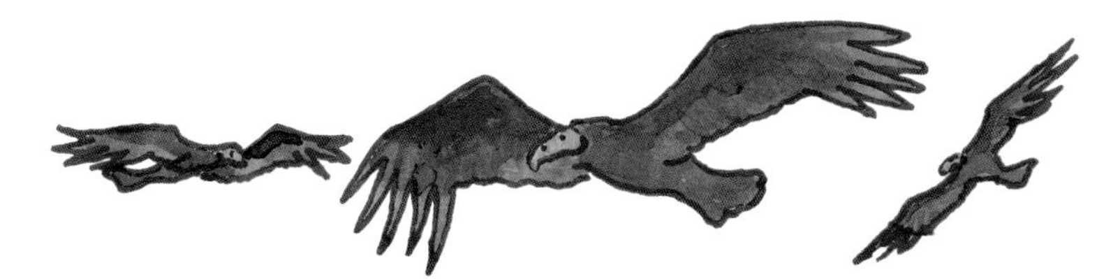

temperatures (global warming); diversion of water resources (to stock tanks and towns and by dams); the rapid growth of human habitat expansion (cities and towns); the introduction of invasive species; pollution and herbicide spraying; industries (farming, ranching, oil extraction, and mining); human actions like hunting, poaching, and collecting native plants and animals; and off-road vehicle use are serious problems we have to deal with to allow deserts to survive.

The animals and plants that live in an ecosystem are interconnected and need each other. Some bats are pollinators for plants like cacti and agave. Deserts are homes to more types of bumblebees, which we need for food and flowers, than anywhere else in the world, but they are declining too. The animals and plants in desert habitats depend upon, connect with, and support each other in their communities. If one species dies or disappears, it affects many other aspects of that ecosystem. And extinct is forever.

In this book, we will learn about North American deserts. You can see where they are located on the map: the Sonoran Desert, the Mojave Desert (which includes Death Valley), the Great Basin Desert, the Chihuahuan Desert, and the Painted Desert.

We will explore these deserts in a 24-hour day and discover their particular geological properties and which remarkable creatures live in each. You can find, name, and count the animals you see during the day, and then the ones that come out after the sun has set. Look carefully! Some like to hide.

Although most of these deserts suffer from many of the same problems, some have unique situations. We will learn about these issues, how they are happening, and what you can do to help save our deserts. You can make a difference. It is very important that we all care about these irreplaceable special places and the living creatures that call them home.

Day is breaking in the **Mojave Desert,** the highest, driest, and smallest of the four main North American deserts, found in parts of California, Nevada, Utah, and Arizona. It's called a "High Desert" because of its altitude, averaging between 3,000 feet (915 meters) and 6,000 feet (1,830 meters). There are a variety of habitats here, from mesas to salt flats and sand dunes. The surrounding mountains block most rain–one California town, now deserted, once went almost two years without a drop of rain. There are several ghost towns in the Mojave–besides little rain, long hot summers, and cold winters, the desert can have winds above 50 mph, so it can be

difficult to live in. But big cities like Las Vegas and Los Angeles spill out into the desert, bringing highways, power lines, military bases, hunting, mining, livestock grazing and farming, and off-road vehicles, destroying animal and plant habitats and using precious water.

FIND THE FOLLOWING CREATURES IN THIS PICTURE:

1 Ladder-Backed Woodpecker; 1 Desert Tortoise; 1 Antelope Squirrel; 1 Desert Hairy Scorpion; 7 Harvester Ants; 1 Raven; 2 Mojave Dotted-Blue Butterflies; 1 Coachwhip (Red Racer); 4 Turkey Vultures; 3 Tarantula Hawk Wasps; 1 Fringe-Toed Lizard; 1 Scott's Oriole; 1 Chuckwalla; 1 Western Patchnose Snake; 1 American Kestrel; 1 Long-Nosed Leopard Lizard

Morning has arrived in the **Great Basin Desert**, the largest and most northern desert in the United States. Spread across valleys and mountains (some over 13,000 feet), it's located mainly in Nevada, but also in California, Idaho, Oregon, Utah, and Arizona, occupying approximately 160,000 square miles. It's a high, cold desert, with a short growing season in the spring, a dry summer, and a cold winter. Most precipitation comes down as snow, not rain. Although rapidly developing cities like Las Vegas, Reno, and Salt Lake City border and affect it, the Great Basin itself is one of the most sparsely populated regions in the United States, so direct human impacts

aren't as pervasive as in some other deserts. But there are widespread indirect effects: more wildfires reducing animal habitats, invasive plants altering the ecosystem, and global warming pushing sagebrush higher so alpine mountain habitats are reduced.

FIND THE FOLLOWING CREATURES IN THIS PICTURE:

1 Golden Eagle; 1 Collared Lizard; 1 Porcupine; 1 Mormon Cricket; 1 Antelope Squirrel; 1 Great Basin Wood Nymph; 1 Black-Billed Magpie; 3 Sage Grouse; 6 Pronghorn Antelope; 1 Bighorn Sheep; 1 Yellow-Bellied Marmot; 1 Pygmy Rabbit; 1 Great Basin Fritillary Butterfly; 1 Coyote; 1 Raven; 1 Great Basin Gopher Snake

To the east, it's now high noon in the **Chihuahuan Desert,** the largest of all North American deserts. Most of it is in Mexico, but portions extend into Texas, New Mexico, and Arizona. In Big Bend (part of the desert) in southwest Texas, you'll find more bird species than in any other North American national park. Summers in the Chihuahuan are long and hot, but because of its high elevation–half is above 4,000 feet (1,220 meters)–winters can turn freezing cold. There are many issues that are causing damage to this magnificent desert. Most large desert creatures, including bison, big cats, and pronghorns, have almost disappeared, and black bears are

totally gone because of hunting or the loss of acceptable habitats. Additional problems include overgrazing by cattle, sheep, and goats; mining (copper, gypsum, salt, lime, sand); and oil and gas drilling.

FIND THE FOLLOWING CREATURES IN THIS PICTURE:

1 Desert Spiny Lizard; 2 Horned Toads; 1 Western Rattlesnake; 4 Javelinas; 1 Burrowing Owl; 1 Harris's Hawk; 1 Turkey Vulture; 2 Monarch Butterflies; 5 Scaled Quails; 1 Collared Lizard; 1 Giant Desert Centipede; 1 Greater Roadrunner; 1 Yucca Moth; 1 Garter Snake; 1 Mexican Ground Squirrel

In the midafternoon light, the **Painted Desert** glows. It's easy to see how it got its name. Color is everywhere, in bands with vibrant hues like yellow, red, pink, blue, and lavender. Sometimes described as "multicolored layer cakes," these patterns are due to minerals in the rocks. For example, limonite creates yellow stripes, hematite red stripes, and gypsum white stripes. There's also a blue section. The Painted Desert is a wind- and water-sculpted expanse of badland hills, flat-topped mesas, and buttes. Beginning near the Grand Canyon, it stretches northeast in Arizona for over 160 miles and includes parts of the Petrified

Forest, continuing north into the Navajo Nation. As in the other deserts we are learning about, here too some species, mainly large animals like pronghorns and bighorn sheep, are dwindling.

FIND THE FOLLOWING CREATURES IN THIS PICTURE:
1 Burrowing Owl; 1 Bark Scorpion; 1 Collared Lizard; 3 Pronghorn Antelope; 1 Western Meadowlark; 3 Pipevine Swallowtail Butterflies; 1 Striped Skunk; 1 Prairie Falcon; 1 Greater Roadrunner; 1 Side-Blotched Lizard; 1 Bighorn Sheep; 1 Plateau Striped Whiptail

The sun streaks across the **Sonoran Desert** in late afternoon. It is really hot! In summer the temperature can reach a sizzling 120°F (49°C), and during the winter it rarely gets below freezing. The Sonoran stretches through California and Arizona, and continues into Mexico. It's one of the richest areas or birds–over 350 kinds–including many hummingbirds. Sadly, some birds, like the little cactus ferruginous pygmy owl and the desert nesting bald eagle, are starting to disappear. This desert is home to sixty species of mammals, but there are almost no Mexican gray wolves left, and a jaguar is very rarely seen. Why are some of these creatures becoming

extinct? Mostly because of human activities, like hunting, and ecosystem-disrupting actions like mining, overgazing, off-road vehicle use, pipeline and huge power line construction, and the encroachment of cities, which build roads, divert water resources, and pollute.

FIND THE FOLLOWING CREATURES IN THIS PICTURE:

1 Antelope Squirrel; 1 Giant Hairy Scorpion; 5 Velvet Ants; 3 Coati; 1 Elf Owl; 1 Gila Woodpecker; 1 Arizona Coral Snake; 1 Cactus Wren; 4 Turkey Vultures; 1 Collared Lizard; 5 Gambel's Quail; 1 Sonoran Whipsnake; 1 Red-Tailed Hawk; 1 Costa's Hummingbird; 1 Desert Tortoise; 3 Painted Lady Butterflies; 1 Greater Roadrunner; 1 Desert Spiny Lizard

Evening is coming to **Death Valley** in the northern part of the Mojave Desert. This is one of the hottest places on earth, with the highest recorded temperature in the Western Hemisphere and maybe the world: 134°F (56.7°C). Not only is this place really hot, it's extremely dry, with an average rainfall of less than two inches. Many early travelers got lost here, and even perished, which is how, in the 1850s, Death Valley got its name. When rain falls in the surrounding mountains, salt washes out and ends up on the valley floor, creating "salt flats." There are also sand dunes, canyons, badlands, rocky ridges, and a few spring-fed wetlands. Perhaps the most destructive human activity

here has been over 150 years of mining (often open-pit and strip mining) for borax, gold and silver, antimony, copper, lead, zinc, and tungsten. Although most mining has stopped in the last few decades, some politicians are trying to reopen Death Valley now for more mining.

FIND THE FOLLOWING CREATURES IN THIS PICTURE:

1 Rock Wren; 3 Gambel's Quail; 1 Bighorn Sheep; 1 Desert Cottontail; 1 Kit Fox; 1 Scorpion; 1 Desert Iguana; 3 Turkey Vultures; 3 Western Pygmy Blue Butterflies; 1 Red-Tailed Hawk; 1 Chuckwalla; 1 Round-Tailed Ground Squirrel; 1 Coachwhip (Red Racer); 1 Zebra-Tailed Lizard; 1 Greater Roadrunner; 1 Side-Blotched Lizard; 1 Tarantula

It is dusk here now in the **Chihuahuan Desert**. Night is arriving. Voracious eaters abound, like the pallid bat, devouring grasshoppers, scorpions, and large crickets. The landscape is dotted with desert shrubs (bushes like creosote), mesquite trees, and lots of cacti–particularly prickly pears. To keep cool, a prickly pear cactus will angle the direction of its green pads to cut down on exposure to the sun. Another plant, the resurrection plant, curls into a tight brown disc when it's dry. Hours after a rain, stems unroll and it opens and turns green. In the spring, after a rare shower, the desert fills up with wildflowers, like

a multicolored quilt. But at night, creatures like the banner-tailed kangaroo rat, the kit fox, and the burrowing owl are more and more rare because of habitat changes, mainly brought on by human behavior

FIND THE FOLLOWING CREATURES IN THIS PICTURE:
1 Western Spotted Skunk; 5 Mexican Free-Tailed Bats; 1 Porcupine; 2 Desert Cottontails; 1 Western Rattlesnake; 1 Desert Banded Gecko; 1 Trapdoor Spider; 1 Giant Desert Centipede; 1 Black-Tailed Jackrabbit; 1 Stink Beetle; 1 Burrowing Owl; 1 Coyote; 1 Hairy Desert Scorpion; 1 Kit Fox; 1 Kangaroo Rat; 1 Whip Scorpion; 1 Yucca Moth; 2 White-Tailed Deer

As night comes to the **Sonoran**, lots of animals like coyotes, owls, and mice come out of their homes and burrows. Bats visit organ pipe cactus flowers that open at night. No other desert on earth has such a variety of plants–over 2,000 different kinds. The giant saguaro cactus grows slowly–only six inches in ten years!–but can reach 50 feet (15 meters) tall and live over 200 years (you see it here with an elf owl's nest in a cavity). The spiniest plant of them all is the teddy bear cholla. Other unusual plants are the ocotillo (which, after a rainfall, sprouts red flowers at the tops of its tall skinny stems), yuccas (which have pointy leaves that hurt if you get

stuck!), and fishhook barrel cacti that lean toward the sun. Many of these special desert plants depend upon insects, birds, bats, and other desert creatures to pollinate them. The animals need the plants for moisture, food, shade, a home, and much more. They need each other.

FIND THE FOLLOWING CREATURES IN THIS PICTURE:

1 Gila Monster; 1 Tarantula; 1 Elf Owl; 2 Spotted Bats; 1 Ringtail; 2 Desert Cottontails; 1 Desert Tortoise; 1 Great Horned Owl; 1 Coyote; 1 White-Lined Sphinx Moth; 1 Desert Banded Gecko; 1 Arizona Coral Snake; 1 Giant Hairy Scorpion; 1 Sonoran Green Toad; 1 Stink Beetle; 1 Bailey's Pocket Mouse; 1 Desert Shrew; 1 Black-Footed Ferret

At night in the **Painted Desert**, Townsend's big-eared bats and the occasional kit fox may be seen, but both species are in decline. A great horned owl silently flies by, looking for a tiny mouse that has come out from its burrow. Barren and austere, the Painted Desert is actually considered a grassland ecosystem rather than a desert, but it's very arid and has little vegetation. It sometimes has noise pollution, day and night, in certain areas, depending upon which way the wind is blowing. You can hear traffic (a "hum") from the distant interstate highway or a train on the railroad tracks to the south, and, overhead, aircraft flyovers. However, off-road travel

is not allowed here at any time, and at night no cars at all are allowed. During the day, vehicles cannot stop on the paved park road and idle their motors for more than two minutes (up to five minutes in bad weather).

FIND THE FOLLOWING CREATURES IN THIS PICTURE:
1 Giant Desert Centipede; 1 Kangaroo Rat, 11 Pallid Bats; 1 Coyote; 1 Black-Tailed Jackrabbit; 1 Tarantula; 1 Bark Scorpion; 1 Great Horned Owl; 3 Canyon Mice; 1 Desert Shrew; 1 Bushy-Tailed Woodrat; 1 Painted Desert Glossy Snake; 1 Bobcat

Midnight in the **Great Basin**. Because of its remote location, away from the light pollution caused by cities and towns, and its cold, clear, almost cloudless skies, this desert is one of the best places in America for stargazing. Don't expect to see many cacti, and don't look for a lot of flowers–just sagebrush, rocks and mountains, and trees like pine, spruce, juniper, and fir. An introduced invasive (not native) plant called cheatgrass is highly flammable and increases the incidence of fire. Human activities like mining have led to heavy metal pollution, cattle grazing has diminished native grasses, and hunting threatens the population of fur-bearing animals.

The Great Basin has less of a variety of animals and plants than any of the other deserts in the Northern Hemisphere, and creatures like the red fox, the gray wolf, the Sierra Nevada bighorn sheep, the desert tortoise, and the southwestern willow flycatcher are seldom seen now.

FIND THE FOLLOWING CREATURES IN THIS PICTURE:

1 Tarantula; 1 Desert Woodrat; 4 Townsend's Big-Eared Bats; 1 Western Rattlesnake; 1 Great Basin Spadefoot Toad; 1 Sierra Nevada Red Fox; 5 Mule Deer; 1 Black-Tailed Jackrabbit; 3 Desert Cottontails; 1 Coyote; 1 Mountain Lion; 1 Kangaroo Rat; 2 Pocket Mice

The moon is going down in the **Mojave Desert**. In a couple hours, nocturnal creatures like bats, mice, and insects including tarantulas and scorpions will return to their burrows and crevices to hide for the hot day coming. Almost a quarter of the plants in the Mojave Desert are unique to it–found nowhere else in the world. The most famous is the Joshua tree, the tall spiny yucca you see in these paintings. Human activity is altering or destroying some of these special plants and animals. A few of the mammals affected are little pocket gophers, bighorn sheep, mountain lions, and Townsend's big-eared bats. Birds disappearing include bald eagles, California brown pelicans,

and cute little Mexican spotted owls. Even reptiles like Coachella Valley fringe-toed lizards and desert tortoises are in trouble, as well as amphibians (lowland leopard frog) and fish (Colorado pikeminnow, humpback chub, and razorback suckers) living in the rare streams or lakes.

FIND THE FOLLOWING CREATURES IN THIS PICTURE:
1 Yucca Moth; 1 Desert Hairy Scorpion; 1 Black-Tailed Jackrabbit; 2 California Leaf-Nosed Bats; 1 Tarantula; 1 Coyote; 2 Desert Cottontails; 2 Pocket Mice; 1 Desert Tortoise; 1 Mojave Desert Sidewinder; 1 Desert Woodrat; 1 Pocket Gopher; 1 Bobcat; 1 Kangaroo Rat; 1 Desert Spider Beetle; 1 Kit Fox

The horizon lightens now in **Death Valley**. Another day dawns in one of the hottest places in the world. Despite such extreme conditions, more than 1,000 plant varieties live in Death Valley–many specially adapted for living in salty soil, like pickleweed and saltbush. Some plants have roots that go straight down ten times the height of a person to collect water. Some have a root system just below the desert floor that spreads out in all directions searching for moisture. You'll find the lowest land in North America here, called Badwater Basin, almost 300 feet below sea level. There are a few isolated springs or creeks–the tiny bright blue native Devils Hole pupfish that lives in some of them

is endangered. The desert tortoise is rare too. In extreme temperatures, it can burrow down into the earth three to five feet to make its underground home. Death Valley, like our other deserts, is a unique, almost magical place...a special part of our world.

FIND THE FOLLOWING CREATURES IN THIS PICTURE:
1 Desert Shrew; 4 Pallid Bats; 1 Bobcat; 2 Desert Cottontails; 1 Pocket Mouse; 1 Scorpion; 1 Sidewinder; 1 White-Lined Sphinx Moth; 1 Black-Tailed Jackrabbit; 2 Desert Banded Geckos; 1 Kangaroo Rat; 1 Stink Beetle; 1 Badger; 1 Kit Fox; 1 Tarantula; 1 Amargosa Toad; 1 Coyote

MOJAVE DESERT
Fun Facts

The **fringe-toed lizard** can dash over sand up to 15 mph. To keep sand out, it has special nasal valves that can close, earflaps, protective eyelids, and a recessed jaw. It dives down into the loose sand in the dunes and "swims" down to cooler depths where it can stay buried for a long time, breathing air trapped in the tiny spaces between the grains of sand.

When threatened, the **chuckwalla** sneaks into crevices between rocks, inflates its body by gulping air, and stays wedged in the small space so tightly it can't be pulled out by a predator.

There are **cockroaches** in the desert—they live underground in the

ANSWERS: DAY

1) 1 Ladder-Backed Woodpecker; 2) 1 Desert Tortoise; 3) 1 Antelope Squirrel; 4) 1 Desert Hairy Scorpion; 5) 7 Harvester Ants; 6) 1 Raven; 7) 2 Mojave Dotted-Blue Butterflies; 8) 1 Coachwhip (Red Racer); 9) 4 Turkey Vultures; 10) 3 Tarantula Hawk Wasps; 11) 1 Fringe-Toed Lizard; 12) 1 Scott's Oriole; 13) 1 Chuckwalla; 14) 1 Western Patchnose Snake; 15) 1 American Kestrel; 16) 1 Long-Nosed Leopard Lizard

sandy soil where it is cool, and they can absorb water through the damp sand.

To protect itself from the strong sun, the **white-tailed antelope squirrel** shades itself with its bushy tail.

In very hot weather, some creatures, like the **western tortoise** and **vulture,** urinate on their legs–the evaporation cools them off.

Harvester ants dig maze-like tunnel systems in the soil, sometimes as deep as fifteen feet down. They store the seeds they collect in grain rooms. There are other rooms too, like nurseries to develop larvae and nurture eggs.

ANSWERS: NIGHT

1) 1 Yucca Moth; 2) 1 Desert Hairy Scorpion; 3) 1 Black-Tailed Jackrabbit; 4) 2 California Leaf-Nosed Bats; 5) 1 Tarantula; 6) 1 Coyote; 7) 2 Desert Cottontails; 8) 2 Pocket Mice; 9) 1 Desert Tortoise; 10) 1 Mojave Desert Sidewinder; 11) 1 Desert Woodrat; 12) 1 Pocket Gopher; 13) 1 Bobcat; 14) 1 Kangaroo Rat; 15) 1 Desert Spider Beetle; 16) 1 Kit Fox

GREAT BASIN DESERT

Fun Facts

A **gray fox** can climb fifty feet up a limbless tree trunk. Then it can jump from limb to limb, like a cat or a squirrel, to escape from predators.

There are a dozen or so species of rattlesnakes in North American deserts. The **western diamondback** is the largest and can grow up to seven feet in length. It rattles with its strong tail muscles when it feels threatened. A new segment in the tail is formed every time the snake molts.

Some animals, like **spadefoot toads**, estivate (sleep) during the hottest, driest months. And in cold deserts, some animals hibernate, or sleep through the winter, in a protected place.

Snakes don't have ears but are sensitive to ground vibrations, so they can feel danger or even the approach of dinner!

Bats are the only mammals that can truly fly. To "see" at night, they use a form of sonar–they

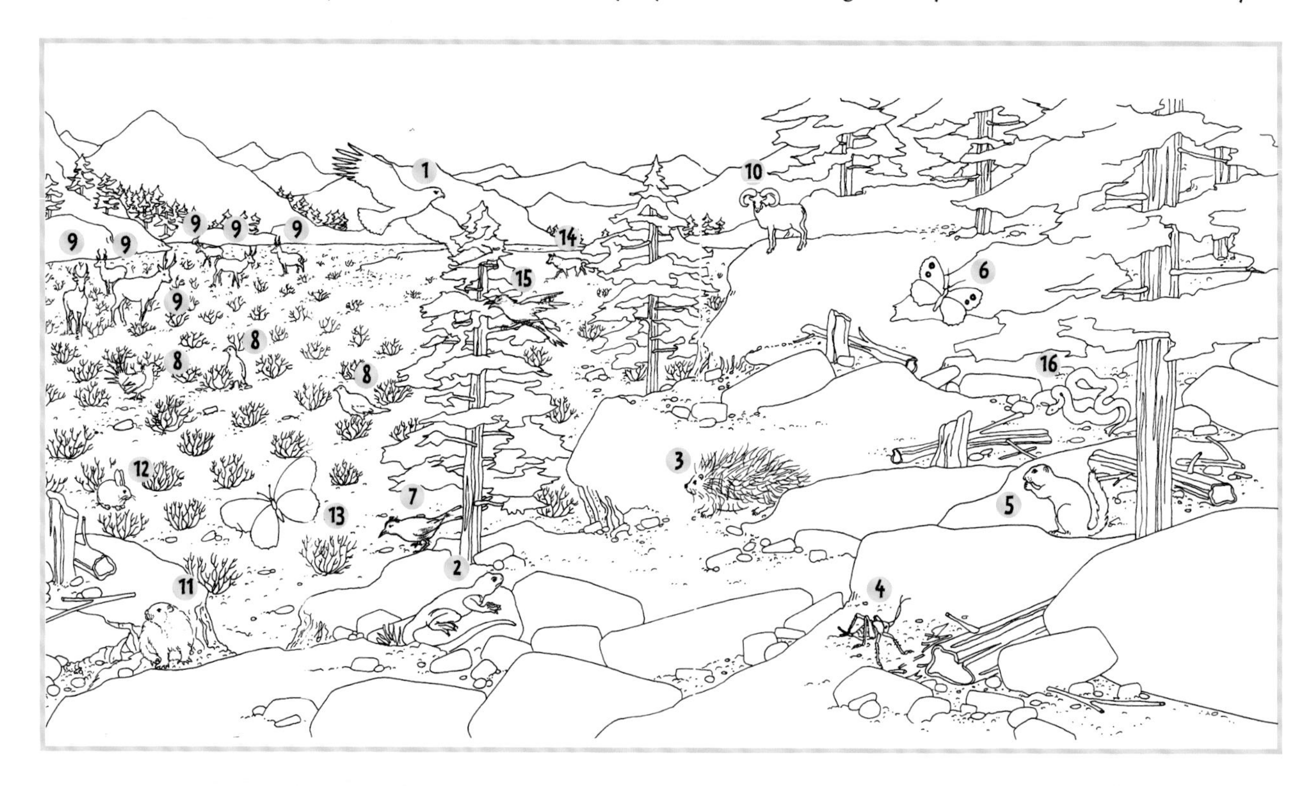

ANSWERS: DAY

1) 1 Golden Eagle; 2) 1 Collared Lizard; 3) 1 Porcupine; 4) 1 Mormon Cricket; 5) 1 Antelope Squirrel; 6) 1 Great Basin Wood Nymph; 7) 1 Black-Billed Magpie; 8) 3 Sage Grouse; 9) 6 Pronghorn Antelope; 10) 1 Bighorn Sheep; 11) 1 Yellow-Bellied Marmot; 12) 1 Pygmy Rabbit; 13) 1 Great Basin Fritillary Butterfly; 14) 1 Coyote; 15) 1 Raven; 16) 1 Great Basin Gopher Snake

send out a sound and listen for it to bounce off objects. They like to sleep hanging upside down, and although most live about ten years, some species can live to be thirty.

The **woodrat** is called a pack rat because it collects all kinds of items for its nest, like bones, sticks, dung, leaves, and other small objects found in deserts—even coins, keys, or jewelry if you drop them!

Bighorn sheep are known for head-to-head combat between males, which can last for more than twenty-four hours. A ram's horns grow longer every year; they can weigh up to thirty pounds, as much as the rest of the body bones combined. They have two toes on each foot, which can spread wide for support and have rough pads so they can grip the ground and travel around uneven rocky terrain.

ANSWERS: NIGHT

1) 1 Tarantula; 2) 1 Desert Woodrat; 3) 4 Townsend's Big-Eared Bats; 4) 1 Western Rattlesnake; 5) 1 Great Basin Spadefoot Toad; 6) 1 Sierra Nevada Red Fox; 7) 5 Mule Deer; 8) 1 Black-Tailed Jackrabbit; 9) 3 Desert Cottontails; 10) 1 Coyote; 11) 1 Mountain Lion; 12) 1 Kangaroo Rat; 13) 2 Pocket Mice

CHIHUAHUAN DESERT

Fun Facts

Javelinas (also called collared peccaries or vaquira) can eat cactus with spines because they have tough leather-like skin around their mouths and their digestive system can pass sharp objects through. They walk single file, one after another, when traveling.

The **horned lizard** (or horned toad) can squirt a jet of blood from ducts in the corner of its eye up to three feet away to startle attackers. These small lizards blend in with the background and are often hard to see.

Termites and **ants** are particularly abundant in the warm Chihuahuan and Sonoran deserts—they often outnumber all other animals combined.

ANSWERS: DAY

1) 1 Desert Spiny Lizard; 2) 2 Horned Toads; 3) 1 Western Rattlesnake; 4) 4 Javelinas; 5) 1 Burrowing Owl; 6) 1 Harris's Hawk; 7) 1 Turkey Vulture; 8) 2 Monarch Butterflies; 9) 5 Scaled Quails; 10) 1 Collared Lizard; 11) 1 Giant Desert Centipede; 12) 1 Greater Roadrunner; 13) 1 Yucca Moth; 14) 1 Garter Snake; 15) 1 Mexican Ground Squirrel

The **giant desert centipede** can grow to six or eight inches long, but it usually has only about forty legs, not one hundred.

When disturbed, the **stink beetle** puts its rear end up into the air and a nasty smelly liquid comes out.

Cartoon-looking **roadrunners** can run up to 15 mph. Their long tails act like a brake, stopping them suddenly, or like a rudder–by flicking them to one side, they can turn in mid-stride.

ANSWERS: NIGHT

1) 1 Western Spotted Skunk; 2) 5 Mexican Free-Tailed Bats; 3) 1 Porcupine: 4) 2 Desert Cottontails; 5) 1 Western Rattlesnake; 6) 1 Desert Banded Gecko; 7) 1 Trapdoor Spider; 8) 1 Giant Desert Centipede; 9) 1 Black-Tailed Jackrabbit; 10) 1 Stink Beetle; 11) 1 Burrowing Owl; 12) 1 Coyote; 13) 1 Hairy Desert Scorpion; 14) 1 Kit Fox; 15) 1 Kangaroo Rat; 16) 1 Whip Scorpion; 17) 1 Yucca Moth; 18) 2 White-Tailed Deer

PAINTED DESERT
Fun Facts

Scorpions and **large spiders** have "book lungs." Folds in the abdomen, like pages in a book, provide surfaces for gas exchange to the tissues and are helpful in preventing water loss.

The **pronghorn antelope** is one of the fastest animals in North America–like a car, it can sprint up to 60 mph!

There are more **lizards** in North American deserts than any other animal.

The largest desert spider is the fuzzy **tarantula**. Its leg span can be six inches across–bigger than your hand. There are about twenty different kinds of tarantulas in the Southwest US. They can live to be thirty years old.

ANSWERS: DAY

1) 1 Burrowing Owl; 2) 1 Bark Scorpion; 3) 1 Collared Lizard; 4) 3 Pronghorn Antelope; 5) 1 Western Meadowlark; 6) 3 Pipevine Swallowtail Butterflies; 7) 1 Striped Skunk; 8) 1 Prairie Falcon; 9) 1 Greater Roadrunner; 10) 1 Side-Blotched Lizard; 11) 1 Bighorn Sheep; 12) 1 Plateau Striped Whiptail

Tiny **kangaroo rats** never need to drink water. They get moisture from the insects, plants, and seeds they eat. Specialized kidneys allow the disposal of waste with very little loss of water. These small creatures are often seen crossing roads at night, balancing with their furry tails as they hop on strong elongated hind legs. A kangaroo rat can jump up to ten feet in a single bound and swing its rudder-like tail to rapidly change direction.

Coyotes howl at night to let other coyotes know where they are. They travel a long way to hunt and have great eyesight, a keen sense of smell, and excellent hearing. They are found in all of the deserts in this book.

ANSWERS: NIGHT

1) 1 Giant Desert Centipede; 2) 1 Kangaroo Rat; 3) 11 Pallid Bats; 4) 1 Coyote; 5) 1 Black-Tailed Jackrabbit; 6) 1 Tarantula; 7) 1 Bark Scorpion; 8) 1 Great Horned Owl; 9) 3 Canyon Mice; 10) 1 Desert Shrew; 11) 1 Bushy-Tailed Woodrat; 12) 1 Painted Desert Glossy Snake; 13) 1 Bobcat

SONORAN DESERT

Fun Facts

Gila woodpeckers make holes in saguaro trunks. Each year, after they raise their young, they abandon their home, and other animals like elf owls, bats, lizards, pack rats, and mice move in.

A **ringtail** isn't a cat–it's a member of the raccoon family. A good climber, it can turn its hind feet backward and, using sharp claws to grasp onto the bark, go headfirst down a tree trunk.

The **cactus wren** builds a football-sized nest (made of grass stems and lined with feathers) in the crook of a saguaro arm or spiny cholla cactus. They don't get hurt by cactus spines because they have bony feet and a thick coat of feathers.

ANSWERS: DAY

1) 1 Antelope Squirrel; 2) 1 Giant Hairy Scorpion; 3) 5 Velvet Ants; 4) 3 Coati; 5) 1 Elf Owl; 6) 1 Gila Woodpecker; 7) 1 Arizona Coral Snake; 8) 1 Cactus Wren; 9) 4 Turkey Vultures; 10) 1 Collared Lizard; 11) 5 Gambel's Quail; 12) 1 Sonoran Whipsnake; 13) 1 Red-Tailed Hawk; 14) 1 Costa's Hummingbird; 15) 1 Desert Tortoise; 16) 3 Painted Lady Butterflies; 17) 1 Greater Roadrunner; 18) 1 Desert Spiny Lizard

The **elf owl** is the smallest owl in the world–only five inches high, it could fit in the palm of your hand. It lives in old woodpecker holes in saguaro cacti and eats centipedes, insects, and even scorpions. Before feeding a baby owl a scorpion, the mom rips the stinger off.

The **Gila monster** is the largest and the only poisonous lizard in the US. The poison comes through grooves in its teeth–it bites down and grinds its jaws to kill prey. It eats as much as possible and stores extra food in its fat tail.

ANSWERS: NIGHT

1) 1 Gila Monster; 2) 1 Tarantula; 3) 1 Elf Owl; 4) 2 Spotted Bats; 5) 1 Ringtail; 6) 2 Desert Cottontails; 7) 1 Desert Tortoise; 8) 1 Great Horned Owl; 9) 1 Coyote; 10) 1 White-Lined Sphinx Moth; 11) 1 Desert Banded Gecko; 12) 1 Arizona Coral Snake; 13) 1 Giant Hairy Scorpion; 14) 1 Sonoran Green Toad; 15) 1 Stink Beetle; 16) 1 Bailey's Pocket Mouse; 17) 1 Desert Shrew; 18) 1 Black-Footed Ferret

DEATH VALLEY
Fun Facts

The **desert iguana** is darker when it is cold to absorb warm sunlight, and when its body temperature rises, it becomes lighter to reflect the sun.

The **red racer** is also called a coachwhip snake–not poisonous, but it's fast, and it bites!

Scorpions get enough water from eating and digesting their prey; they don't have to drink.

When threatened by a predator, some **desert geckos** can "drop," or amputate, their own tail. But the dropped tail doesn't just lie there–it can make movements (swing back and forth, and flip up in the air) for up to half an hour, to distract the predator.

Turkey vultures have great eyesight and a keen sense of smell.

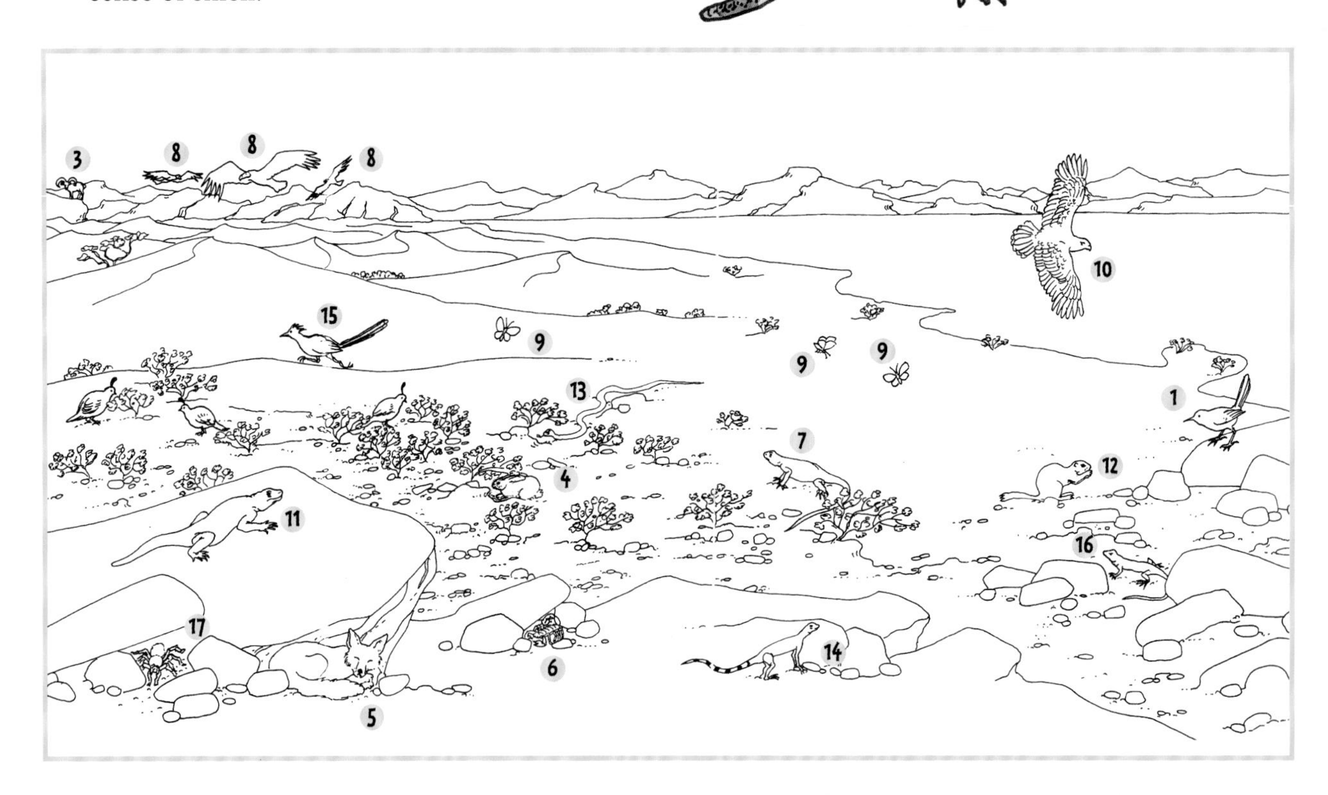

ANSWERS: DAY

1) 1 Rock Wren; 2) 3 Gambel's Quail; 3) 1 Bighorn Sheep; 4) 1 Desert Cottontail; 5) 1 Kit Fox; 6) 1 Scorpion; 7) 1 Desert Iguana; 8) 3 Turkey Vultures; 9) 3 Western Pygmy Blue Butterflies; 10) 1 Red-Tailed Hawk; 11) 1 Chuckwalla; 12) 1 Round-Tailed Ground Squirrel; 13) 1 Coachwhip (Red Racer); 14) 1 Zebra-Tailed Lizard; 15) 1 Greater Roadrunner; 16) 1 Side-Blotched Lizard; 17) 1 Tarantula

Sidewinder rattlesnakes move fast along hot dunes, propelling themselves head forward and dragging their body behind to minimize contact with the hot sand and provide traction.

Do you know why many animals in hot deserts (like the **jackrabbit, mule deer**, and **kit fox**) have large ears? Because blood circulating in the ears helps keep the animal cool.

Some small creatures, like **beetles** and **lizards**, reduce the amount of heat they absorb from the desert surface by having long legs to keep them high up and to disperse heat. Pale-colored fur and feathers help others to keep cool by reflecting sunlight.

ANSWERS: NIGHT

1) 1 Desert Shrew; 2) 4 Pallid Bats; 3) 1 Bobcat; 4) 2 Desert Cottontails; 5) 1 Pocket Mouse; 6) 1 Scorpion; 7) 1 Sidewinder; 8) 1 White-Lined Sphinx Moth; 9)1 Black-Tailed Jackrabbit; 10) 2 Desert Banded Geckos; 11) 1 Kangaroo Rat; 12) 1 Stink Beetle; 13) 1 Badger; 14) 1 Kit Fox; 15) 1 Tarantula; 16) 1 Amargosa Toad; 17) 1 Coyote

HOW YOU CAN HELP!

In this book, we've learned about North American deserts, our beautiful but fragile ecosystems. They are home to so many unique animals and plants that are now in trouble.

You've read about ways that climate change and other man-made challenges are impacting these important habitats. There is a lot you can do to help the desert and its creatures survive and thrive.

First, maybe you love animals. Gray wolves are decreasing in the southwest deserts. You can adopt a gray wolf virtually from the Arizona-Sonora Desert Museum or the World Animal Foundation. Through the World Wildlife Fund, you can also adopt other rare desert creatures, like a reclusive red fox, a cute pygmy rabbit, or a ringtail. The Game, Fish, and Wildlife departments of several states (such as California, Nevada, and Arizona) help you adopt a real desert tortoise that can live with you. What about bees? As major pollinators of all sorts of plants, they are incredibly important to so much we, and millions of animals, need for life, like food! But they are dying all over the world. The Sonoran Desert alone has over 700 species of bees, many whose very existence is in danger. The Tucson Bee Collaborative explains how you can help: plant native plants, nurture clumps of flowers, have a diversity of flowers for a diversity of bees, and keep soil nesting places bare.

You have probably experienced or heard in the news about "extreme weather events," like forest fires, floods and mudslides, excessive heat, hurricanes and tornadoes, water contamination, and droughts. These extremes are most likely due to global climate change caused by human activity. Most deserts are naturally hot and have little water, but even deserts are not used to such extreme conditions. To cool down,

animals sometimes have to move further up mountainous slopes where it is colder. They may have to burrow deeper, affecting their breathing and eating habits. Some creatures' lives are so disrupted that their entire species is starting to disappear and go extinct. Desert plants are affected too. Many are slow-growing, so are hard to replace. Some die out, or, like the animals, try to migrate up to higher, cooler desert areas.

You can help by reducing the amount of energy you use, which contributes to climate change. You probably know some of these tricks, but they all make a difference: If it's cold out, don't keep the heat in your home too high. Put on a sweater and wear socks to stop using too much energy. If you go to a drive-through and there's a line, ask if you can park and go inside, rather than keeping the car running and using fuel while you wait in line. Walk or ride a bike when you can, instead of getting a ride in a car. Make sure the light bulbs in your home are all the new compact fluorescent lights (CFLs) which use much less energy. And reducing your water use is helpful too. Turn off the tap when you are brushing your teeth. Take shorter showers or baths with less water in them.

Other problems in the desert have come as cities have expanded into desert regions, causing light pollution and diverting precious water supplies. Farming with fertilizers and pesticides changes soil chemistry, and ranching with herds of goats and cattle creates problems with overgrazing. Hunting of animals and collecting plants is an issue.

Mining and oil and gas production, as well as off-road recreational vehicles, damage deserts. Pipelines and giant electric cables stretch across delicate desert areas.

Damage to these fragile ecosystems can be prevented. The organization Defenders of Wildlife works hard to protect wild animals and their homes, including trying to limit the use of recreational vehicles that are destroying habitats in the Mojave Desert. Through their organization, you can become a Biodiversity Ambassador–if you are new to activism, you start out at the "Desert Tortoise Level."

Some nature organizations make it easy to learn how to become politically active. They even have sample letters you can write to politicians, and give you the addresses to send them to. The National Park Service has all sorts of fun programs–for Girl Scouts, Boy Scouts, artists, and citizen scientists of all ages.

Finally, it's thrilling to see dark skies, full of stars. If you've seen the Milky Way at night, you know it's exciting and beautiful. These days though, in most places in America, you can no longer see many stars at night. There is too much light pollution, caused by humans in cities, from traffic and even their own houses. But in Death Valley in the Mojave Desert, you can still stargaze. You can see the night sky as it was millions of years ago. It is a Dark Sky Park, one of the last places in America where you can really see the universe.

You can help with light pollution. Tell your family or school to install lighting only

when and where it is needed. Point light fixtures down, rather than up, and shield them. Use timers and motion sensors on outdoor lights. Get rid of outdated or inappropriate light fixtures. Visit a Dark Sky Park. Join the International Dark-Sky Association and get educated.

There are many more things you, your school, and your family can do to help preserve America's deserts and the fascinating plants and animals that live there. Get creative! It can be fun, and you will be doing important work. The living creatures–animals and plants–in America's deserts will be thankful, as will future generations of young people, like you.

Organizations You Can Contact

International Dark-Sky Association: https://www.darksky.org/get-involved/

Sierra Club: https://www.sierraclub.org/take-action

Arizona-Sonora Desert Museum: http://www.desertmuseum.org/adoptions/animal.php?s=wolf

Adopt a Gray Wolf: https://gifts.worldwildlife.org/gift-center/gifts/Species-Adoptions/Gray-Wolf

Adopt a Desert Tortoise
In California: https:// www.tortoise.org/cttc/adoption.htm

In Nevada: https://tortoisegroup.org/desert-tortoise-adoption-program/

In Arizona: https://www.desertmuseum.org/programs/tap.php

The Nature Conservancy: https://preserve.nature.org/page/80352/action/1

Tucson Bee Collaborative: https://www.inaturalist.org/projects/tucson-bee-collaborative

Defenders of Wildlife: https://defenders.org/wild-places/deserts

National Park Service: https://www.nps.gov/getinvolved/volunteer.htm

Take action to protect animals and natural habitats beyond your home:
https://www.worldanimalprotection.org/take-action]
https://www.rewild.org/

Glossary (Words You Should Know)

Camouflage: Patterns, shapes, or colors that help an animal blend into its surroundings and hide from predators.

Carnivore: A meat eater; an animal that eats the flesh of another animal.

Cold-blooded: An animal whose temperature changes with its surroundings (warmed by the sun or chilled in the cold).

Diurnal: Active during the day.

Ecosystem: A community of living things in a specific physical environment. It can be as large as our planet, or as small as a pond, with particular species of living things. Soil, water, altitude, temperature, and precipitation (rain or snow), as well as animal and plant life, define an ecosystem.

Forage: To hunt or search for food.

Habitat: The natural home of an animal, such as a forest, park, grassland, ocean, or desert.

Herbivore: An animal that eats plants; a vegetarian.

Hibernate: When an animal remains inactive during cold months, often "sleeping" in a burrow or cave.

Indigenous: Living or occurring naturally in a particular location; native or original to an area.

Invasive: An organism (animal or plant) that causes ecological or economic harm in a new environment where it is not native.

Mammal: A warm-blooded animal that usually has fur or hair and feeds its young with milk. Humans, dogs, and mice are mammals.

Migrate: To travel on a regular or seasonal journey to make a nest, find food, or mate.

Nocturnal: Active at night and asleep during the day.

Predator: An animal that hunts other animals for food.

Reptile: Cold-blooded vertebrates, like snakes, turtles, and lizards.

Species: A particular type of animal or plant.

Territorial: When a creature prefers and defends a particular area from others.

Venomous: Able to inflict a sting or bite to deliver chemicals, like poison, that can kill or paralyze other animals.

Vertebrates: Animals with backbones. Reptiles, birds, fishes, and humans are vertebrates.